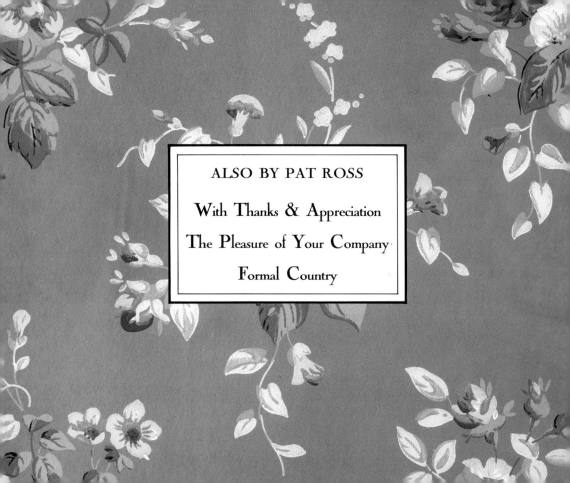

ALSO BY PAT ROSS

With Thanks & Appreciation

The Pleasure of Your Company

Formal Country

With Love and Affection
on your 25th Anniversary

To _Larry and Jan_

From _John and Carolyn_

All love is sweet,
Given or returned. Common as light is love,
And its familiar voice wearies not ever. . . .
They who inspire it most are fortunate,
As I am now; but those who feel it most
Are happier still.

—*Prometheus Unbound*
Percy Bysshe Shelley
1818–1819

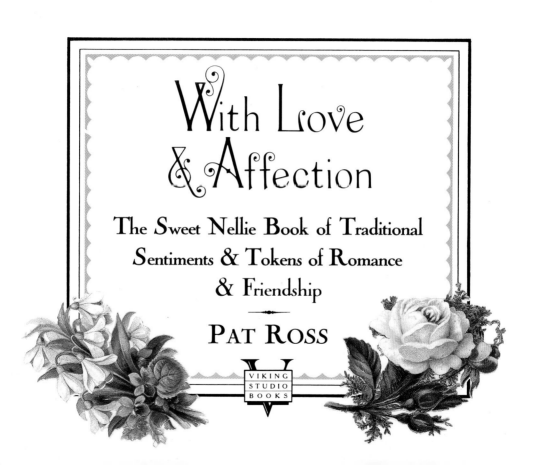

With Love & Affection

The Sweet Nellie Book of Traditional Sentiments & Tokens of Romance & Friendship

PAT ROSS

VIKING
STUDIO
BOOKS

VIKING STUDIO BOOKS
Published by the Penguin Group
Viking Penguin, a division of Penguin Books USA Inc.,
40 West 23rd Street, New York, New York 10010, U.S.A.
Penguin Books Ltd, 27 Wrights Lane, London W8 5TZ, England
Penguin Books Australia Ltd, Ringwood, Victoria, Australia
Penguin Books Canada Ltd, 2801 John Street, Markham, Ontario, Canada L3R 1B4
Penguin Books (N.Z.) Ltd, 182–190 Wairau Road, Auckland 10, New Zealand

Penguin Books Ltd, Registered Offices: Harmondsworth, Middlesex, England

First published in 1990 by Viking Penguin, a division of Penguin Books USA Inc.

1   3   5   7   9   10   8   6   4   2

Copyright © Pat Ross, 1990   All rights reserved

ISBN 0-670-83058-5

CIP data available

Printed in Japan   Set in Nicholas Cochin
Designed by Amy Hill

AN APPRECIATION

With each new book, there are many colleagues, friends, and family members to thank once again. My sincere appreciation both to those who contributed their time and expertise and those who made up the support section. Particular gratitude goes to the following people: Leisa Crane, for her research and good cheer (for the third time) on this series; the enthusiastic staff at Sweet Nellie; Berta Montgomery, for the lovely vintage wallpaper, which never seems to run out; the many ephemera dealers—Marjorie Adams, Bernice Stewart, and Bonnie Ferris, especially—who hunted through their files for us; Carolyn Gore, for lending her family's friendship albums for this book and others; the many librarians and antiquarian booksellers who were never too busy to answer endless questions and search the stacks with us; Amy Berkower, my agent; Joel and Erica; and, of course, everyone at Viking Studio Books, most particularly Michael Fragnito, Barbara Williams, Emily Kuenstler, and Amy Hill for coming through on a schedule that only angels could keep!

INTRODUCTION

Despite the profusion of mass-produced greetings and valentines, the child in all of us still treasures the colorful bits of paper, the candy hearts, and the glitter that make a handmade creation special. I can remember unwrapping the white paper doilies from the local 5 & 10 when I was young, and praying I could paste my stiff paper hearts in the center of those perfect doilies without smearing even one. Soon my fingers were crusty from dotting on the homemade flour-and-water paste. It took hours to think up clever or wicked (the greater challenge!) verses for the recipients.

Thinking up verses of love and friendship gave our forebears great pleasure. Their well-chosen words, composed for life's every occasion, were sweet and gentle. And if poetry did not come easily, there were the countless verse-and-posy "guides" of the day, filled with appropriate sentiments. Their hand-embellished calling cards offered words of fidelity and love; their valentines were layered with every imaginable image of devotion; their secret notes of affection, penned in perfect calligraphy, were made to be tucked into a hand or a pocket. Nineteenth- and early-twentieth-century etiquette books poured forth with advice on everything from hand-holding to proper courtship behavior. The many missives and paper tokens from yesteryear have become today's cherished keepsakes.

Our fast-paced lives leave little time for waxing eloquent on paper when we wish to let special people know we care about them. Times have changed, but others' words, selected with enormous care, have meaning still. It is these words and sentiments that fill this little book.

Romantic
Notions

The weather is usually fine while people are courting. . . .

—*Virginibus Puerisque*
Robert Louis Stevenson
1895

Love, indeed, lends a precious seeing to the eye, and
hearing to the ear: all sights and sounds are glorified by
the light of its presence.

—*Salad for the Solitary and the Social*
Frederick Saunders
1871

Between two fires

By this dear relenting kiss,
I'd no anger in my thought;
Come, my love, by this and this,
Let our quarrel be forgot.

—Verse from a
nineteenth-century
calling card

Each kiss a heart-quake,—for a kiss's strength
I think, it must be reckon'd by its length.

—*Don Juan*, canto the second, clxxxvi
George Gordon, Lord Byron
1819

ove has been compared to debt: both keep their captives awake at night, and in a perpetual state of unrest during the day.

—*Salad for the Solitary*
and the Social
Frederick Saunders
1871

"**W**on't you come into the garden? I would like my roses to see you."

—*The Perfect Hostess*
Rose Henniker Heaton
1931

Love is a deep well from which you may drink often, but into which you may fall but once.

—*"Dame Curtsey's" Book of Novel Entertainments for Every Day in the Year*
Ellye Howell Glover
1907

CUPID

His wing is the fan of a lady.
His foot is an invisible thing;
And his arrow is tipped with a jewel,
And shot from a silver string.

—Verse from a
nineteenth-century
calling card

Although Cupid cannot be said to be young, he seems to enjoy perpetual youth, for he is not in the least the worse for wear—his locks are still golden, his cheeks glowing, and the bright kindling glance of his eye is radiant as ever.

—*Salad for the Solitary
and the Social*
Frederick Saunders
1871

I thought to undermine the heart
By whispering in the ear.
— *"The Siege of a Heart"*
Sir John Suckling, (1609–1642)

Love me,
love my dog.

—A proverb from
the time of
Saint **B**ernard
1090–1153

"Whatever be in
life your lot.
I ask of you
forget me not."

Remember
Me

Oh! love is such a strange affair;
So strange to all.
   It cometh from above
   And lighteth like a dove
            On some.
   But some it never hits
   Unless it give them fits.
            Oh, hum.

—*The Album Writer's Friend*
J. S. Ogilvie
1881

Man's love is like Scotch snuff—
You take a pinch and that's enough.
Profit by this sage advice,
When you fall in love, think twice.

—*The Album Writer's Friend*
J. S. Ogilvie
1881

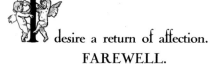 desire a return of affection.
FARELL.

> —Verse from a
> nineteenth-century
> calling card

Within that breast so good so pure
If compassion ever loved to dwell
Pity the sorrows I endure.
The cause thou know'st full well
The grief that on my quiet preys
That rends my heart that checks my tongue
I fear will last me all my days,
But feel it will not last me long.

—Verse from a
nineteenth-century
calling card

HE LOVES ME:
HE LOVES ME NOT

Daisy! each petal
My fortune may settle,—
Soon, late, or never:
Now, then, for ever,
Give me a token!
One little word
Unuttered, but heard:
One little sigh,—
One glance of an eye:

I'll take it as spoken.
Soon, late, or never:
Tall, short, or clever:
Never, for ever,
Which shall it be?
Daisy, tell me?
Am I heart-broken?

—*The Quiver of Love*
1876

UNCHANGEABLE

My heart shall be
The faithful compass
That still points to thee.

—Verse from a
nineteenth-century
calling card

TRUE LOVE

Thus hand in hand
Through life we'll go
Through checkered paths
Of joy and woe.
We have loved on earth;
May we love in heaven.

—Verse from a
nineteenth-century
calling card

Affection's
links of steel
so true
Must never
rust twixt
me and
you.

Etiquette of Love

THE LETTER OF LOVE

This is a letter that is controlled altogether by the heart, and the feelings of that vital part are the best criterion to go by; but let the style of the letter be simple and sincere, and whether it should be long or short depends entirely on what is to be said.

—*Perfect Etiquette: Or How to Behave in Society*
n.d.

April 4 - 1914

Dear Doris:—
I will miss you when I get away up in Vermont, but I will not forget you, and will send you some pretty post cards as I go from place to place
Your friend
P. T. Pomeroy

Miss Doris Jardine.
4 Main St,
Potsdam
N.Y.

If you are engaged, of course you should write a love letter——the most beautiful that you can——but don't write baby-talk and other silliness that would make you feel idiotic if the letter were to fall into strange hands.

—*Etiquette*
Emily Post
1923

Be the wind and weather foul or fine,
Still, lovely Nelly, I am thine!

—Letter from Matthew Matson
to Nelly Primrose

If Matthew's heart be just and true,
His Nelly's heart will be so too.

—Letter, in reply, from Nelly
to Matthew

It should be remembered, that the same means which were used to gain affection, are absolutely necessary to preserve it; and I think an indelicate behavior and gross familiarity, if they do not alienate affection, never fail to quench desire. . . .

Sobriety, prudence, good nature, a virtuous disposition, a good understanding, and a competent fortune, are qualities never to be dispensed with in this matter.

—*The Lover's Instructor: Or
The Whole Art of Courtship
Rendered Plain and Easy*
1809

*A*ll the world loves a lover—but this does not keep the world from watching closely and criticizing severely any breach of good manners. . . . Any public display of affection anywhere at any time is grossly unrefined. Love is sacred, and it should not be thrown open to the rude comments of strangers.

—*Book of Etiquette*
Lillian Eichler
1922

*O*ne word spoken in haste may inflict a wound in the heart of your companion which will require months or years to heal over.

—*American Etiquette*
and Rules of Politeness
A. E. Davis
1882

Consider not the gift of the lover, but the love of the giver.

—"Dame Curtsey's" Book of
Novel Entertainments
for Every Day in the Year
Ellye Howell Glover
1907

It is always best to give something of your own production or discovery. If the recipient has any love for you, the value of the gift will be enhanced many fold by being the offspring of your effort and skill.

—*American Etiquette
and Rules of Politeness*
A. E. Davis
1882

With Love's Fond Greeting

For beauty and riches I do not pine,
I ask a heart that responds to mine.

With fondest

LOVE
TO THEE

Be My
Valentine

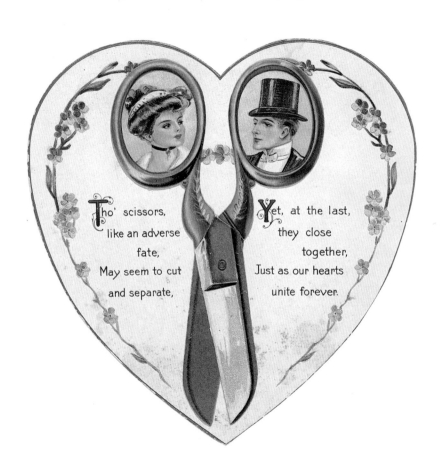

Tho' scissors,
like an adverse
fate,
May seem to cut
and separate,

Yet, at the last,
they close
together,
Just as our hearts
unite forever.

When we dwell on the lips of the lass we adore,
  Nor a pleasure in nature is missing:
May his soul be in heaven: he deserved it, I'm sure,
  Who was the first inventor of kissing.

With this rose accept my love

Fly, my sweet, and beauteous dove,
  Bear this letter to my love;
Winged messenger, with care,
  Bring my answer from the fair:
A heart that's constant still is mine
Lovely, lovely Valentine.

My Heart greets you.

—*Carvalho's Polite Valentine
    Writer: Or The Lover's Repository
    for the Present Year*
    182–

To one I love

When we dwell on the lips of the lass we adore,
  Nor a pleasure in nature is missing:
May his soul be in heaven: he deserved it, I'm sure,
  Who was the first inventor of kissing.

Fly, my sweet, and beauteous dove,
  Bear this letter to my love;
Winged messenger, with care,
  Bring my answer from the fair:
A heart that's constant still is mine
Lovely, lovely Valentine.

—Carvalho's Polite Valentine
  Writer: Or The Lover's Repository
  for the Present Year
  182—

To one I love

My heart to you is given:
oh, do give yours to me;
We'll lock them up together,
and throw away the key.

—*Salad for the Solitary and the Social*
Frederick Saunders
1871

FROM A BOOK-BINDER

My pretty volume, neatly bound,
 In you these truths I see,
You're witty, wise, and virtuous too,
 The very wife for me:
As you are single, and so am I,
 Suppose we bind together,
And thus one handsome Folio make,
 And shine in gold and leather.
O take me to those arms of thine,
Like paper white, my Valentine.

—*Cupid's Delight*
Nineteenth century

TO A BAKER

You knead your dough, I need your love—
   Let both our needs in one combine
No more to fondness crusty prove
   But be my well-bread Valentine.

—Dick's Original Album
Verses and Acrostics
1879

INSCRIPTIONS FOR WEDDING RINGS

A token sent with true intent

As endless is my love as this

As God saw fitt our knot is knitt

Bee true in heart

Hearts united live contented

I will ever love the giver

In thy sight is my delight

Yours I am assuredly

—*Ye Garland of Ye Sette
of Odd Volumes*
James Roberts Bronn
1883

**L** apis lazuli

O pal

V erd antique

E merald

M alachite

E merald

—On the arrangement
 of gems in a ring
 *Finger-Ring Lore:
 Historical, Legendary,
 Anecdotal*
 William Jones
 1890

I do not repent I gave my consent
This circle, though but small about
The devil, jealousy, shall keep out

—*Finger-Ring Lore:
 Historical, Legendary,
 Anecdotal*
 William Jones
 1890

Friendship's Offering

Real friendship is a slow grower; and never thrives unless engrafted upon a stock of known and reciprocal merit.

—*Good Manners*
1870

When friendship once
Is rooted fast
It is a plant
No storm can blast.

—Verse from a
nineteenth-century
calling card

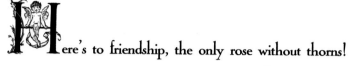

Here's to friendship, the only rose without thorns!

—*Prosit:*
A Book of Toasts
1904

May friendship, like wine, improve as time advances,
And may we always have old wine, old friends, and young cares.

Friendship is a
sheltering tree.

Keep thy friend
Under thy own life's key.

—*"Dame Curtsey's" Book
of Novel Entertainments
for Every Day in the Year*
Ellye Howell Glover
1907

Fate gives us parents; choice gives us friends.

—*Prosit:
A Book of Toasts*
1904

Go, little book, thy destined course pursue,
Collect memorials of the just and true,
And beg of every friend so near
Some token of remembrance dear.

Let not our friendship be like the rose, to sever;
But, like the evergreen, may it last forever.

Accept my friend these lines from me,
They show that I remember thee,
And hope some thought they will retain
Till you and I shall meet again.

—*The Album Writer's Friend*
J. S. Ogilvie
1881

It seems fitting that a book about traditions of the past should be decorated with period artwork. In that spirit, the art in *With Love & Affection* has been taken from personal collections of original nineteenth- and early-twentieth-century calling cards, tokens of affection, etchings, valentines, and other paper treasures of the time.

 The endpapers and chapter openings contain patterns reproduced from some of our favorite vintage wallpapers.